The Future of AI-Powered Business Taxes

Automated Compliance, Digital Audits & Zero-Friction Accounting

By Joe Correa

Published by Live Stronger Faster

This book is for educational and informational purposes only. The author and publisher are not engaged in rendering legal, financial, tax, or other professional advice. Readers should consult a qualified professional before making any financial decisions.

First Edition

Table of Contents

Introduction 5

Chapter 1: The Rise of the Autonomous Tax System 11

Chapter 2: Real-Time Tax Intelligence and Predictive Compliance 19

Chapter 3: Digital Governments, AI Tax Authorities, and the End of Paperwork 25

Chapter 4: Blockchain, Smart Contracts, and the Tax Ledger of the Future 30

Chapter 5: Zero-Friction Accounting and the End of Financial Bottlenecks 36

Chapter 6: Predictive Profit, Continuous Optimization, and the AI CFO 42

Chapter 7: The Autonomous Enterprise and the Disappearance of Financial Fear 48

Chapter 8: From Compliance to Competitive Advantage: How AI Turns Taxes Into Power 55

Chapter 9: Resilience by Design: How AI Builds Tax-Safe, Shock-Proof Businesses 62

Chapter 10: The Zero-Friction Economy: Where Taxes, Accounting, and Business Fully Disappear Into Intelligence 70

Final Thoughts 78

Introduction

The future of business taxation is no longer something that belongs to tomorrow—it is already unfolding around us in real time, reshaping how companies calculate, report, defend, and optimize their taxes at a speed and precision that would have seemed impossible just a decade ago. Artificial intelligence is rapidly becoming the invisible engine behind global financial systems, and in the world of business and corporate taxation, its impact is even more profound. What once required teams of accountants, tax attorneys, auditors, and compliance officers is now increasingly handled by machine-driven systems that operate continuously, analyzing millions of data points, detecting patterns, flagging risks, and optimizing outcomes in ways humans simply cannot replicate. In this final book of the AI Business & Corporate Tax Optimization series, we explore not only how AI already governs modern tax infrastructure, but how it will soon transform taxation into a fully automated, real-time, self-correcting digital ecosystem. This future is not about filing a tax return once a year—it is about tax systems that update every day, compliance that happens in the background, audits that are predictive rather than punitive, and businesses that operate with near-zero tax friction because every transaction is automatically categorized, validated, and optimized by intelligent software.

Across the previous nine books, you have learned how AI already controls tax preparation, expense tracking, audit defense, bookkeeping, payroll, compliance, multi-state filings, financial forecasting, and strategic structuring, but Book 10 looks ahead to the inevitable next phase: a world where taxation becomes almost invisible to business owners because it is embedded directly into every financial action they take. Instead of scrambling at year-end, AI-driven systems will calculate your tax liability in real time as you invoice customers, pay vendors, hire employees, or move money between accounts. Governments will no longer rely on manual reporting because they will receive verified financial data instantly through encrypted digital tax networks. Businesses will no longer fear audits because compliance will be continuously validated by AI, leaving no gaps for errors or surprises. This is the age of digital tax infrastructure, where software replaces paperwork, algorithms replace guesswork, and data replaces delays. Those who understand this transformation will thrive with unprecedented efficiency and profit protection, while those who ignore it will find themselves increasingly locked out of the financial system, buried in penalties, or unable to compete.

The most powerful shift AI brings to business taxation is not just automation—it is the replacement of reactive compliance with proactive intelligence. In the old world, companies reported what already happened and hoped it was correct. In the new world, AI models simulate what will happen before it happens, predicting cash flow, tax liabilities, compliance risks, and audit probabilities long before a transaction is finalized. These systems can instantly compare millions of tax rules, court decisions, and regulatory updates across jurisdictions to determine the most efficient and compliant way to structure every business move. When you open a new subsidiary, enter a new state, sell internationally, or change your payroll structure, AI will instantly model the tax impact and suggest the optimal path forward. This is not theory—these systems are already being deployed by governments, multinational corporations, and financial institutions. The future belongs to businesses that plug into these AI tax engines and allow them to guide every financial decision with mathematical certainty rather than human intuition.

One of the most important developments in AI-powered taxation is the rise of digital audit systems, where compliance is no longer enforced by random IRS letters but by continuous algorithmic verification. Instead of audits that occur years after mistakes are made, AI-driven tax authorities will validate transactions as they happen, flagging inconsistencies instantly and resolving them before they grow into penalties or legal exposure. Businesses will operate in a transparent yet secure environment where tax data is cryptographically verified, automatically reconciled, and constantly cross-checked against banking systems, payment processors, payroll platforms, and blockchain-based records. This will eliminate the gray areas that currently cause so much stress for entrepreneurs and corporations alike. When AI is monitoring compliance in real time, you no longer wonder if something was recorded correctly—it either is or it isn't, and the system tells you immediately.

At the same time, AI will dramatically shift the balance of power between businesses and governments by making tax optimization more accessible, precise, and defensible than ever before. Instead of relying on expensive tax attorneys or complex strategies that may or may not survive an audit, companies will use AI to generate legally sound, regulator-approved optimization strategies based on continuously updated tax law databases. These systems will know exactly which deductions, credits, depreciation schedules, and entity structures apply to your business model, industry, location, and growth stage. They will adjust those strategies in real time as laws change, revenue fluctuates, or new opportunities appear. This creates a future where even small businesses and startups can access the same tax intelligence once reserved for Fortune 500 corporations, leveling the financial playing field in a way that fundamentally reshapes entrepreneurship. Perhaps the most revolutionary change of all will be the disappearance of traditional tax filing altogether. In the future, there will be no annual tax season in the way we know it today. Instead, businesses will operate inside always-on tax platforms that calculate, collect, and remit taxes automatically as income is earned and expenses are incurred. Sales tax, payroll tax, corporate income tax, VAT, and international withholding will all be handled seamlessly through AI-driven financial rails. Governments will receive their revenue instantly, businesses will never fall behind, and financial records will always be up to date. This eliminates late fees, penalties, and the fear of compliance mistakes because everything is processed by software that never sleeps, never forgets, and never guesses.

For business owners, this new world offers something even more valuable than convenience—it offers clarity. When AI manages your taxes, you always know exactly where you stand financially. You can see your true profit after tax in real time. You can test scenarios before making decisions. You can expand into new markets with confidence. You can scale without fear that tax complexity will crush your growth. In this environment, taxation stops being a burden and becomes a strategic tool that you can use to maximize reinvestment, protect cash flow, and build long-term wealth. This is why understanding the future of AI-powered business taxes is not optional—it is a core survival skill for anyone who plans to compete in the digital economy. This book will guide you through what this future looks like, how it is being built right now, and how you can position your business to take full advantage of it. You will learn how digital tax systems, AI compliance engines, automated audits, real-time reporting, and predictive financial models will converge into a single intelligent tax ecosystem. You will see how governments are restructuring their tax authorities around data and algorithms, and how businesses are shifting from reactive compliance to continuous optimization. Most importantly, you will discover how to prepare your company for this transition so you are not disrupted by it, but empowered by it.

As the final chapter in the AI Business & Corporate Tax Optimization series, this introduction sets the stage for a world where taxation becomes frictionless, transparent, and strategically aligned with business success. The age of paperwork, panic, and post-mortem compliance is ending. The age of intelligent, automated, and predictive tax systems has begun. Those who understand this transformation will build faster, safer, and more profitable companies than ever before. Those who do not will find themselves trapped in outdated systems that no longer serve the modern economy. This book is your roadmap to the future—where AI does not just file your taxes, but actively helps you build, protect, and multiply your business wealth in a fully digital financial world.

Chapter 1

The Rise of the Autonomous Tax System

The modern tax system is undergoing the most dramatic transformation in its history, and at the center of that transformation is artificial intelligence. For more than a century, business taxation has been driven by paperwork, human judgment, and delayed reporting cycles that forced companies to operate with incomplete financial visibility. Today, that entire model is collapsing. AI is replacing periodic filing with continuous financial intelligence, turning tax compliance into a living, real-time system that constantly measures, verifies, and optimizes every financial event as it happens. In an autonomous tax environment, every invoice, payroll run, vendor payment, depreciation entry, and international transfer is automatically classified, validated, and synced with regulatory frameworks without human intervention. What once took weeks of bookkeeping and months of tax preparation is now accomplished in milliseconds by algorithms that never sleep, never forget, and never miscalculate.

This shift is not just about convenience; it is about control. In a traditional system, business owners operate in the dark, guessing how much tax they owe until accountants finalize reports long after the year has ended. AI replaces that uncertainty with continuous financial truth. Autonomous tax engines calculate real-time tax exposure, cash flow, and compliance status at every moment, giving business leaders the ability to make informed decisions instantly. Whether a company is considering hiring new staff, purchasing equipment, expanding into a new state, or launching a global e-commerce operation, AI can model the exact tax impact before the decision is made. This predictive power fundamentally changes how businesses grow, allowing them to optimize structure, timing, and investment strategy with mathematical precision instead of intuition.

Governments are also embracing this new model because it creates a more accurate, transparent, and efficient tax system. Instead of relying on self-reported data that may be incomplete or incorrect, tax authorities increasingly receive verified transaction data directly from financial platforms, banks, payroll providers, and point-of-sale systems. AI cross-checks these streams in real time, detecting discrepancies immediately and resolving them before they become enforcement cases. The result is a world where audits become rare, fraud becomes difficult, and compliance becomes a built-in feature of the financial system rather than a burden placed on business owners. This benefits both sides: governments collect revenue faster and more reliably, while businesses eliminate the fear of surprise penalties and retroactive audits.

At the heart of the autonomous tax system is machine learning trained on massive bodies of tax law, court rulings, regulatory guidance, and historical filings. These models do not simply follow static rules; they learn how tax authorities interpret those rules in practice. This means they can predict not just what the law says, but how it will be enforced. When a business classifies an expense, claims a deduction, or structures a transaction, AI evaluates how that decision would be viewed in an audit, calculating risk scores and compliance probabilities instantly. This creates a new standard of tax certainty where companies know, in advance, whether their strategies will hold up under regulatory scrutiny.

Another critical component of the autonomous tax system is continuous reconciliation. Every financial transaction is instantly matched across multiple data sources—bank accounts, credit cards, payroll records, inventory systems, invoicing platforms, and tax ledgers. If anything does not match, AI flags it and corrects it immediately. This eliminates the accumulation of errors that traditionally plague businesses and cause major problems at tax time. In this environment, financial records are always clean, always current, and always defensible. Business owners no longer scramble to find receipts, reconstruct transactions, or justify decisions made months earlier because everything has already been documented and verified by software.

As this system matures, it will also integrate directly with government tax platforms through secure digital channels. Taxes will be calculated, withheld, and remitted automatically based on real-time financial activity. Sales tax, VAT, payroll tax, and corporate income tax will flow continuously rather than in large, stressful quarterly or annual payments. This creates smoother cash flow for businesses and eliminates the shock of unexpected tax bills. AI will also manage compliance across multiple jurisdictions, handling the complexity of different state, national, and international rules without manual effort. For global and online businesses, this is a revolutionary shift that removes one of the biggest barriers to expansion.

The rise of autonomous taxation also brings profound strategic advantages. When taxes are calculated in real time, businesses can optimize how and when they earn revenue, incur expenses, and move money. AI can suggest the best timing for investments, the most efficient depreciation schedules, the optimal entity structures, and the most favorable geographic footprints. It can automatically adjust withholding and estimated payments to minimize overpayment while avoiding penalties. In effect, AI turns taxation into a continuously optimized financial strategy rather than a painful after-the-fact obligation.

Most importantly, the autonomous tax system frees entrepreneurs and executives to focus on growth instead of compliance. Instead of spending hours with spreadsheets, accountants, and government forms, they can rely on AI to handle the complexity of modern taxation with speed, accuracy, and confidence. This is not just a technological upgrade—it is a shift in how businesses experience the financial world. Taxes become predictable, transparent, and manageable, allowing companies to scale faster, take smarter risks, and build long-term wealth without fear of regulatory chaos.

This new reality is arriving faster than most people realize. Fintech platforms, accounting software providers, and government agencies are already laying the groundwork for fully automated tax ecosystems. Blockchain-verified records, real-time reporting APIs, and AI-driven compliance engines are rapidly becoming standard infrastructure. Businesses that adopt these systems early will enjoy a powerful competitive advantage, while those that cling to manual processes will find themselves slower, more expensive to operate, and increasingly exposed to compliance risk. The autonomous tax system is not optional—it is the foundation of the future digital economy.

The Year Taxes Disappeared

In the early days of her logistics startup, Elena remembered tax season as a time of dread. Boxes of receipts, frantic emails to her accountant, late-night spreadsheets, and the constant fear that something had been missed haunted her every spring. But in the tenth year of her business, something strange happened—tax season never arrived. Instead, her financial dashboard simply glowed green every day, showing her real-time profit, real-time tax liability, and real-time compliance status. Her AI system, quietly working in the background, had transformed her company into a living, breathing financial organism that was always in balance. There were no forms to file, no payments to scramble for, and no letters from the tax authority. Everything was already done.

One morning, Elena received a notification that her company was expanding into two new countries through a partnership deal. In the old world, this would have triggered weeks of panic about international tax rules, VAT, transfer pricing, and compliance risks. Instead, her AI assistant instantly simulated the tax impact of the expansion, adjusting her projected cash flow, optimizing the structure of the partnership, and configuring the correct reporting rules for each jurisdiction. By the time Elena finished her coffee, the system had already updated her financial forecasts and compliance settings. The expansion was not just approved—it was already optimized.

Months later, a government audit algorithm scanned Elena's company as part of a routine compliance sweep. In the past, that would have meant months of stress and legal bills. This time, it took less than a second. The AI cross-checked every transaction, payroll record, invoice, and bank transfer against regulatory rules and cleared the company automatically. Elena never even saw the audit happen. Her system simply recorded that her compliance score was perfect and moved on.

As her company grew, Elena noticed something else: she was making better decisions. Because she could see her true after-tax profit in real time, she knew exactly how much she could reinvest, how much she could distribute to herself, and when it made sense to hire or expand. There were no surprises, no hidden liabilities, and no fear of the unknown. Taxes had become just another data stream—important, but never overwhelming.

One evening, while reviewing her financial dashboard, Elena realized that the system had quietly saved her millions of dollars over the years by optimizing depreciation schedules, timing revenue, and structuring transactions in ways she would never have thought of on her own. The AI had become not just her compliance engine, but her financial strategist. It was constantly scanning the global tax landscape, adjusting her business to take advantage of new rules and opportunities as soon as they appeared.

In that moment, Elena understood something profound: taxes had not disappeared—they had been absorbed into intelligence. What used to be a painful, confusing, and risky process had become a smooth, invisible layer of her business operations. The fear was gone. The friction was gone. All that remained was clarity, control, and growth. The future had arrived quietly, and for the first time in her career, Elena felt truly free to build without limits.

Chapter 2

Real-Time Tax Intelligence and Predictive Compliance

The defining characteristic of the AI-driven tax future is not automation alone, but awareness. Real-time tax intelligence transforms taxation from a delayed, reactive process into a continuous, living system that sees, understands, and anticipates every financial event as it occurs. Instead of waiting months to know how much tax is owed or whether a filing was correct, AI platforms now track income, expenses, payroll, asset purchases, cross-border transfers, and regulatory obligations in the moment they happen. This creates a dynamic tax environment where compliance is not something you do later—it is something that exists at all times, embedded into the fabric of daily business operations. Every transaction becomes a data point in a constantly evolving tax model that updates your liabilities, deductions, credits, and risks in real time.

This continuous awareness enables predictive compliance, one of the most powerful capabilities of artificial intelligence in financial regulation. Predictive compliance means the system does not merely check whether something is compliant after the fact—it predicts whether it will remain compliant in the future based on changing laws, evolving enforcement trends, and your business's behavior. If your company is drifting toward a risk zone, AI can detect that pattern long before a regulator ever notices. It can warn you when expense ratios look suspicious, when payroll classifications are drifting out of compliance, when sales tax nexus thresholds are approaching, or when international transactions trigger reporting requirements. Instead of reacting to audits or penalties, businesses are guided away from danger in advance, making compliance proactive rather than defensive.

Real-time tax intelligence also fundamentally changes how businesses plan. When AI continuously models tax outcomes, financial decisions no longer have to rely on outdated reports or best guesses. A CFO can see how today's revenue will impact next quarter's tax bill, how a new hire affects payroll taxes, or how a capital investment will alter depreciation and cash flow. Entrepreneurs can simulate multiple scenarios before committing to a major move, instantly comparing the tax impact of leasing versus buying, operating as an LLC versus an S-corp, or expanding domestically versus internationally. This level of foresight turns taxation into a strategic planning tool instead of a compliance headache.

Governments benefit just as much from this shift. Real-time reporting gives tax authorities unprecedented visibility into economic activity without requiring intrusive audits or manual filings. AI systems receive transaction data directly from financial institutions, payment processors, and business platforms, then reconcile it automatically against tax rules. This reduces fraud, closes loopholes, and improves revenue collection while lowering administrative costs. The system becomes self-enforcing because discrepancies are detected immediately, not years later. For compliant businesses, this means fewer audits and faster issue resolution. For the overall economy, it means a more accurate, fair, and efficient tax system.

One of the most transformative aspects of predictive compliance is how it handles regulatory change. Tax laws evolve constantly, and in the traditional system, businesses often fall out of compliance simply because they are unaware of new rules. AI platforms monitor legislation, court rulings, regulatory guidance, and enforcement actions across jurisdictions, updating compliance models automatically. When a new rule takes effect, the system adjusts how it classifies transactions, calculates liabilities, or flags risks. Businesses no longer have to chase legal updates or worry about missing critical changes—compliance updates happen in the background, silently and instantly.

This creates a future where even the most complex businesses—global e-commerce brands, SaaS companies, remote workforces, digital marketplaces, and multinational enterprises—can operate with confidence. AI handles the complexity of multiple tax codes, currencies, reporting standards, and filing requirements without human bottlenecks. Real-time dashboards show exactly where a company stands in every jurisdiction, how much tax is owed, what has already been paid, and what risks exist. This transparency eliminates surprises and allows leaders to run their organizations with financial precision that was once only possible for the largest corporations.

Predictive compliance also changes the psychology of taxation. When businesses know that their systems are constantly checking and optimizing compliance, fear disappears. There is no longer anxiety about what might happen in an audit because the AI has already tested every transaction against regulatory standards. There is no longer panic about year-end because the numbers are always current. Taxes become predictable, manageable, and integrated into daily operations. This reduces stress, improves cash flow management, and creates a sense of financial stability that empowers businesses to grow faster and more confidently.

As real-time tax intelligence becomes the norm, it will redefine the relationship between businesses and governments. Compliance will no longer be enforced through punishment and retroactive corrections, but through collaboration between intelligent systems that share verified data. This creates a more transparent and trustworthy economic environment where both sides benefit. Businesses get certainty and efficiency. Governments get accuracy and fairness. The old adversarial model of taxation fades away, replaced by a digital partnership built on data, automation, and predictive insight.

The Algorithm That Knew First

When Marcus launched his global design agency, he expected complexity, but he did not expect clarity. His AI finance system gave him a real-time window into every aspect of his company's financial life. He could see revenue flowing in from clients in five countries, payroll being processed for remote designers, and taxes being calculated automatically for every jurisdiction. One afternoon, as Marcus reviewed a potential partnership deal, his AI assistant issued a quiet alert. The system had detected that the proposed revenue structure would trigger an unexpected tax obligation in a foreign market within three months. Without the warning, Marcus would have walked straight into a compliance nightmare.

Instead, the AI proposed an alternative structure that achieved the same business goal with a far lower tax burden and full regulatory compliance. Marcus approved the change with a single click. He never had to consult a lawyer, read a tax code, or worry about missing something. The system had already done the work.

Weeks later, a new regulation was passed that affected how digital services were taxed in one of Marcus's key markets. While his competitors scrambled to understand the change, Marcus's AI had already updated its models. His invoices, reporting, and tax calculations adjusted automatically. He did not even know a law had changed until he saw a note in his dashboard explaining how the system had optimized his compliance strategy.

One day, a client asked Marcus how he managed to scale so smoothly across borders without running into tax problems. Marcus smiled. He realized that his success was not just about creativity or business skill—it was about intelligence embedded into his operations. His AI had become a silent guardian, constantly watching the future and steering his company away from danger before it ever appeared.

Chapter 3

Digital Governments, AI Tax Authorities, and the End of Paperwork

The future of business taxation will not be shaped only by companies adopting artificial intelligence—it will be driven just as powerfully by governments transforming themselves into digital-first, AI-operated tax authorities. Around the world, tax agencies are abandoning slow, paper-based systems and replacing them with machine-driven platforms capable of processing billions of transactions in real time. This is not merely an upgrade to old infrastructure; it is a fundamental redefinition of how governments collect revenue, enforce compliance, and interact with businesses. In the coming decade, the idea of filing a tax return will feel as outdated as sending a fax. Instead, businesses will operate inside fully integrated digital tax networks where compliance is continuous, automatic, and invisibly embedded into every financial transaction.

AI-powered tax authorities are being built on massive data pipelines that connect banks, payroll systems, accounting software, e-commerce platforms, customs agencies, and payment processors into a single financial intelligence grid. Every sale, wage payment, dividend, expense, or international transfer flows through this network, where it is instantly categorized, validated, and matched against tax rules. This eliminates the need for businesses to manually report their activity because the government already has verified, real-time access to the data. Fraud becomes dramatically harder, errors are caught immediately, and revenue collection becomes faster and more accurate than any human-driven system could ever achieve.

One of the most important effects of digital tax authorities is the disappearance of uncertainty. In the traditional system, businesses never truly know whether their filings are correct until years later when an audit might occur. In the AI-driven system, compliance is constantly verified as transactions occur. If something is misclassified or missing, the system flags it immediately and allows it to be corrected on the spot. This creates a world where audits are no longer disruptive events—they become continuous background processes that ensure accuracy without ever interrupting operations. Businesses no longer live in fear of retroactive penalties because problems are fixed in real time.

Digital tax governments also radically reduce administrative costs for both sides. Governments no longer need massive bureaucracies to process forms, chase down errors, or conduct manual audits. Businesses no longer need armies of accountants to prepare filings, reconcile records, and defend against audits. AI handles all of it automatically. This efficiency allows governments to lower compliance burdens while improving revenue collection, and it allows businesses to redirect time and money from paperwork to innovation and growth.

The integration of AI into government tax systems also enables more intelligent policy enforcement. Instead of applying one-size-fits-all rules, AI can evaluate each business in context, understanding industry norms, economic cycles, and behavioral patterns. This allows for smarter enforcement that targets actual risk rather than punishing honest mistakes. For compliant businesses, this means fewer audits and faster resolution of issues. For governments, it means more effective regulation with less friction.

Another major transformation is the global alignment of tax systems. As countries digitize their tax infrastructure, they are building interoperable platforms that allow data to flow securely across borders. This makes it easier to track international income, prevent double taxation, and ensure that multinational businesses pay the correct amount in each jurisdiction. AI acts as the translator between different tax codes, currencies, and reporting standards, making global compliance far simpler than it has ever been before.

As digital governments become the norm, the relationship between businesses and tax authorities will shift from adversarial to collaborative. Instead of submitting reports and hoping they are accepted, businesses will operate inside shared data environments where compliance is continuously validated. Disputes will be resolved quickly with transparent data rather than lengthy legal battles. Trust will increase because both sides see the same verified information.

This does not mean governments become more intrusive—it means they become more efficient. Data is collected automatically from financial systems that businesses already use, eliminating redundant reporting. Privacy and security are protected through encryption and access controls. The result is a tax system that is more accurate, less burdensome, and far more predictable than anything that came before.

In this new world, paperwork disappears, uncertainty fades, and compliance becomes part of the digital fabric of the economy. Businesses that adapt to this reality will operate with unprecedented speed, clarity, and confidence. Those that resist will find themselves struggling to keep up with a system that no longer waits for manual processes. The future of taxation is digital, intelligent, and seamless—and it is arriving faster than most people realize.

The Last Tax Form

When Daniel inherited his family manufacturing company, he also inherited its greatest headache: taxes. Filing season meant chaos—boxes of documents, endless emails, and constant fear of mistakes. But everything changed when his country launched its new AI-powered tax authority. Overnight, Daniel's accounting software connected directly to the government's digital tax network. Every invoice, payroll run, and supplier payment was now verified automatically. There were no forms to submit and no deadlines to remember.

At first, Daniel did not trust it. He kept his old records just in case. But month after month, the system proved itself. Taxes were calculated and paid automatically. Compliance notices arrived instantly if something looked wrong. Audits never happened because the system was always auditing.

One day, Daniel found an old tax return in a filing cabinet—a thick stack of paper from years ago. He realized it was obsolete, a relic of a world where humans had tried to manage complexity with forms and signatures. Now, intelligence did the work. His company was free to grow without fear, and for the first time, taxes were simply part of the background—quiet, accurate, and invisible.

Chapter 4

Blockchain, Smart Contracts, and the Tax Ledger of the Future

The next great leap in AI-powered taxation will come from the fusion of artificial intelligence with blockchain and smart contract technology, creating what can best be described as the global tax ledger. While AI provides intelligence, prediction, and automation, blockchain provides trust, immutability, and verification. Together, they form a financial nervous system that records every economic event with cryptographic certainty, making fraud, manipulation, and misreporting nearly impossible. In this future, every sale, payroll payment, asset purchase, royalty, loan, and investment will be written into a secure, distributed ledger that is accessible to both businesses and tax authorities in real time. This eliminates disputes over what happened, when it happened, and how it should be taxed, because the data itself becomes the single source of truth.

Smart contracts extend this power even further by turning tax rules into executable code. Instead of relying on human interpretation of tax law, governments and financial institutions will encode tax obligations directly into programmable contracts that automatically execute when conditions are met. When a customer makes a purchase, the correct sales tax is instantly calculated, withheld, and transferred to the appropriate tax authority. When payroll is processed, income tax and employment contributions are automatically deducted and reported. When a business sells an asset, capital gains tax is computed and settled immediately. There is no filing, no waiting, and no room for error because the system enforces the rules at the moment of transaction.

This model creates a world where taxation becomes frictionless. Businesses no longer need to track every transaction manually or worry about whether they have complied with the law. The ledger does it for them. Every transaction carries its own tax logic, embedded into the financial fabric of the economy. AI continuously monitors this ledger, analyzing patterns, forecasting liabilities, and optimizing strategies, while blockchain ensures that the records cannot be altered or falsified. Together, they create a system that is transparent, secure, and fair.

One of the most powerful implications of a blockchain-based tax ledger is the elimination of disputes. In the traditional system, disagreements arise because records are incomplete, inconsistent, or manipulated. With a cryptographically secured ledger, every party sees the same data. There is no need to argue over receipts, invoices, or bank statements because the ledger itself is the authoritative record. Audits become simple algorithmic checks rather than invasive investigations, and compliance becomes a matter of mathematics rather than paperwork.

This system also enables real-time settlement of taxes across jurisdictions. For global businesses, this is revolutionary. Instead of navigating dozens of tax agencies, filing deadlines, and reporting formats, transactions are automatically routed through smart contracts that allocate the correct tax amounts to each country, state, or city involved. Transfer pricing, VAT, withholding taxes, and customs duties are calculated and paid instantly based on verified data. AI ensures that the rules are applied correctly, even as laws change, while blockchain guarantees that every party is paid accurately and transparently.

For governments, this creates a level of revenue certainty never before possible. Taxes are collected at the moment economic value is created, eliminating delays, evasion, and administrative waste. Budgets become more predictable. Fraud becomes far more difficult. Enforcement becomes largely unnecessary because the system enforces itself. This allows governments to reduce compliance burdens on businesses while increasing overall tax efficiency. For businesses, the benefits are just as profound. Cash flow becomes smoother because taxes are paid in small, continuous increments rather than large, disruptive lump sums. Financial statements become more accurate because tax liabilities are always up to date. Strategic planning becomes easier because AI can model future tax obligations with unprecedented precision. The entire financial operation becomes cleaner, faster, and more reliable.

Perhaps most importantly, this system creates a new level of trust between businesses and governments. When both sides rely on the same immutable ledger, transparency replaces suspicion. Disputes are resolved by data rather than by lawyers. Compliance becomes a shared goal rather than a constant battle. This fosters a healthier economic environment where innovation and growth are encouraged instead of constrained by bureaucratic friction.

As blockchain and AI converge, the tax system of the future will no longer feel like a separate, external force imposed on businesses. It will become an integrated part of the digital economy, woven into every transaction and every financial decision. The ledger will not just record what happened—it will actively shape how value flows through the global marketplace, ensuring that taxation is fair, efficient, and fully aligned with economic reality.

The Ledger That Never Forgot

When Ava launched her digital marketplace, she never expected taxes to become the simplest part of her business. Every transaction on her platform ran through a smart contract connected to the global tax ledger. Customers paid in multiple currencies, vendors operated in different countries, and yet every tax obligation was handled instantly and invisibly. Ava never filed a return. She never calculated VAT. She never worried about withholding taxes. The ledger did it all.

One morning, a vendor claimed that the platform had overpaid taxes on a large sale. In the old world, this would have led to weeks of arguments and audits. Instead, Ava opened the ledger. Every step of the transaction was there: the sale price, the jurisdiction, the tax rate, the payment, and the transfer to the tax authority. The data was cryptographically verified and shared by all parties. The dispute ended in seconds.

As Ava's business grew, she realized something even more powerful. The ledger was not just keeping records—it was giving her insight. Her AI system analyzed the data to predict cash flow, optimize pricing, and suggest expansion strategies that minimized tax friction. The combination of intelligence and trust allowed her to scale globally without fear. One evening, Ava watched a real-time visualization of her marketplace's financial activity flowing through the ledger. Millions of transactions, each perfectly recorded, each perfectly taxed. For the first time in history, she realized, the economy was becoming truly transparent and fair. The ledger never forgot, never lied, and never made mistakes—and because of that, businesses like hers could finally grow without the shadow of uncertainty.

Chapter 5

Zero-Friction Accounting and the End of Financial Bottlenecks

For generations, accounting has been the bottleneck of business growth. No matter how innovative the product, how aggressive the marketing, or how global the expansion, companies have always been constrained by slow financial systems that lag behind reality. Numbers were reconciled after the fact, errors accumulated silently, and executives were forced to make decisions based on incomplete or outdated information. Artificial intelligence is eliminating this bottleneck entirely. Zero-friction accounting represents a future where financial data flows instantly, accurately, and continuously across every system a business touches. In this world, accounting is no longer a separate function—it becomes an invisible layer embedded into every transaction, decision, and workflow.

Zero-friction accounting begins with the disappearance of manual data entry. AI systems connect directly to banks, payment processors, payroll platforms, inventory systems, invoicing tools, lending platforms, and government portals. Every transaction is captured automatically at the moment it occurs, categorized intelligently, and reconciled against existing records in real time. There are no spreadsheets to update, no receipts to chase, and no end-of-month surprises. The ledger is always complete because it is constantly being written by machines that operate faster and more accurately than any human team ever could.

This real-time synchronization fundamentally changes the nature of financial truth. Instead of discovering errors weeks or months later, discrepancies are detected immediately. If a payment does not match an invoice, if payroll does not align with tax withholdings, or if inventory values drift from sales records, AI flags and resolves the issue instantly. This prevents small mistakes from compounding into major problems and eliminates the chaos that traditionally erupts during audits, financing rounds, or tax filings. Financial records become self-healing systems rather than fragile documents held together by manual reconciliation.

Zero-friction accounting also transforms financial reporting. In the traditional model, reports are static snapshots of the past. By the time they are generated, the business has already moved on. AI replaces these static reports with live financial intelligence. Dashboards update continuously, showing real-time revenue, expenses, margins, cash flow, tax exposure, and compliance status. Executives no longer ask what happened last quarter—they see what is happening right now and what is likely to happen next. This shifts leadership from reactive management to proactive strategy.

Another defining feature of zero-friction accounting is the integration of compliance directly into financial workflows. Tax rules, reporting requirements, and regulatory obligations are encoded into AI systems that apply them automatically as transactions occur. There is no separate compliance phase because compliance is built into the process itself. Sales tax is calculated and remitted automatically. Payroll taxes are withheld and reported instantly. Depreciation schedules adjust dynamically based on asset usage. International transactions trigger the correct reporting and withholding without manual intervention. Accounting and compliance merge into a single seamless system.

This integration eliminates the fear that has long surrounded accounting and taxation. Business owners no longer worry about missing deadlines, misclassifying expenses, or failing to comply with obscure regulations. The AI handles these details continuously, updating itself as laws change and enforcement patterns evolve. This creates a sense of financial confidence that allows entrepreneurs to focus on growth rather than risk mitigation.

Zero-friction accounting also accelerates access to capital. Investors, lenders, and partners no longer need to wait for audited statements or manually prepared reports. They can access verified, real-time financial data through secure digital channels. This reduces due diligence timelines from months to days or even hours. Businesses can raise capital faster, negotiate better terms, and respond to opportunities immediately because their financial data is always ready and trusted.

As businesses scale, zero-friction accounting becomes even more valuable. Complexity no longer increases friction because AI scales effortlessly. Whether a company operates in one city or fifty countries, the system handles additional volume and regulatory complexity without slowing down. Multi-entity structures, intercompany transactions, and cross-border operations are managed automatically, with AI ensuring consistency and compliance across the entire organization. Growth stops being constrained by financial overhead.

At its core, zero-friction accounting represents a philosophical shift. Accounting is no longer about recording history—it is about enabling the future. It becomes a strategic engine that powers decision-making, risk management, and long-term planning. Businesses that adopt this model will operate with unprecedented speed, clarity, and resilience. Those that cling to manual processes will find themselves increasingly unable to compete in a world that moves at digital speed. The end of financial bottlenecks marks the beginning of a new era in business operations. When accounting disappears into the background, what remains is pure execution. Ideas move faster. Capital flows more efficiently. Growth accelerates. Artificial intelligence does not just improve accounting—it removes it as an obstacle entirely, freeing businesses to operate at the true pace of the modern economy.

The Company That Never Waited

When Nathan founded his software company, he believed speed would be his greatest advantage. His product evolved weekly, his team was distributed across continents, and his customers expected instant results. Yet no matter how fast everything else moved, his finances always lagged behind. Every month ended with delays, reconciliations, and uncertainty. He waited for reports, waited for confirmations, waited for answers. Growth felt like driving a race car with the brakes half engaged.

Everything changed the day Nathan migrated his company to a fully autonomous accounting system. At first, the transition felt unsettling. There were no spreadsheets to review, no monthly closings, no familiar rituals. The system simply connected itself to every financial source and began working silently. Transactions appeared instantly. Numbers updated continuously. For the first time, Nathan could see his company clearly, not as a memory of what had happened, but as a living system unfolding in real time.

Weeks later, a potential acquisition opportunity appeared. In the past, Nathan would have hesitated, knowing that financial due diligence alone could take months. This time, he shared secure access to his live financial dashboard. The investors saw everything: revenue streams, margins, customer acquisition costs, tax exposure, and compliance status. There were no questions, no delays, no back-and-forth. The deal moved forward immediately, not because Nathan had explained his numbers well, but because the numbers explained themselves.

As the company expanded, Nathan noticed something subtle but profound. Decisions no longer felt risky. When he hired new employees, the system showed the exact impact on cash flow and taxes in real time. When he launched new pricing models, AI simulated their long-term effects instantly. When a new regulation passed in a foreign market, his system adapted automatically. He was no longer reacting to events—he was moving ahead of them.

One night, while reviewing his dashboard, Nathan realized that he had not worried about accounting in months. There had been no panic, no surprises, no late nights fixing errors. The bottleneck was gone. His company never waited anymore—not for data, not for approvals, not for clarity. In that moment, Nathan understood that true speed was not about moving faster, but about removing everything that slowed you down.

Chapter 6

Predictive Profit, Continuous Optimization, and the AI CFO

For most of modern business history, financial leadership has been reactive by design. Even the best CFOs were constrained by delayed data, incomplete reports, and historical snapshots that described what had already happened rather than what was about to occur. Artificial intelligence changes this reality completely. In an AI-driven financial environment, profit is no longer measured after the fact—it is predicted, modeled, and optimized continuously. Chapter 6 explores the emergence of the AI CFO: an always-on intelligence layer that forecasts outcomes, adjusts strategy in real time, and transforms financial management from hindsight into foresight.

Predictive profit begins with the idea that every financial action carries a future consequence that can be modeled mathematically. Revenue timing affects tax exposure. Expense structure affects cash flow resilience. Hiring decisions affect long-term liabilities. Capital investments affect depreciation, financing costs, and valuation. Traditional accounting systems record these actions but do not understand them. AI systems, by contrast, are trained to see the ripple effects of every decision across time. They simulate thousands of possible futures in seconds, allowing businesses to see not just what *will* happen, but what *could* happen under different conditions. This turns finance into a strategic discipline rather than a reporting function.

The AI CFO operates continuously, ingesting data from every part of the business and the external environment. It monitors sales velocity, customer churn, market conditions, regulatory changes, interest rates, tax rules, and competitive behavior simultaneously. As these variables shift, the system updates profit forecasts, tax projections, and risk models in real time. Leaders are no longer surprised by downturns, cash crunches, or tax spikes because the system has already seen them coming. Warnings appear early, often months in advance, giving businesses time to adjust course calmly and intelligently.

One of the most powerful capabilities of the AI CFO is scenario modeling. Instead of debating strategy based on opinions or assumptions, leaders can test decisions instantly. What happens to profit if prices increase by five percent? How does cash flow change if a new market is entered? What is the long-term tax impact of restructuring the company or changing entity types? AI answers these questions not with guesses, but with probabilistic forecasts grounded in real data and historical patterns. This removes emotion from financial decision-making and replaces it with clarity. Continuous optimization is the natural outcome of predictive intelligence. When AI understands where profit is coming from and where it is leaking, it can automatically adjust operations to improve outcomes. It can recommend changes in pricing, cost structure, supplier relationships, staffing levels, and capital allocation. It can optimize tax strategies dynamically, shifting deductions, credits, and timing to maximize after-tax profit without increasing risk. Over time, the business becomes more efficient not through periodic restructuring, but through constant micro-adjustments guided by data.

This also transforms how businesses manage risk. Traditional risk management relies on static rules and worst-case assumptions. AI-driven systems monitor risk in real time, identifying emerging threats and quantifying their potential impact. If customer concentration increases, if expenses grow faster than revenue, if tax exposure spikes in a particular jurisdiction, or if compliance risk rises, the AI CFO flags it immediately and proposes corrective actions. Risk becomes something that is actively managed rather than passively endured.

Another critical shift is how human leadership interacts with financial intelligence. The AI CFO does not replace executives—it augments them. Instead of spending time assembling reports or debating numbers, leaders focus on interpreting insights and making strategic choices. Finance becomes a collaborative dialogue between human judgment and machine intelligence. This partnership allows companies to move faster with greater confidence because decisions are informed by both experience and data-driven foresight.

As businesses grow more complex, the value of the AI CFO increases exponentially. Multi-entity structures, global operations, remote workforces, and digital revenue streams generate a level of financial complexity that humans alone cannot manage effectively. AI thrives in this environment. It scales effortlessly, maintaining visibility and optimization across the entire organization regardless of size or geography. Growth no longer overwhelms financial systems—it strengthens them.

Ultimately, predictive profit represents a new philosophy of business management. Companies stop asking, "What did we earn?" and start asking, "What will we earn, and how can we improve it right now?" Finance becomes a forward-looking engine that guides every major decision. In this future, the most successful businesses will not be those with the biggest teams or the most capital, but those with the most intelligent financial systems. The AI CFO becomes the quiet force behind sustained profitability, resilience, and long-term value creation.

The Quarter That Never Surprised Anyone

When Isabel accepted the role of CEO at a fast-growing logistics company, she inherited a familiar problem disguised as success. Revenue was climbing, customers were expanding globally, and headcount was growing rapidly—but no one could clearly explain where the profit was actually coming from. Every quarter ended with surprises. Sometimes they were pleasant. Often they were not. Cash flow dipped unexpectedly. Taxes spiked without warning. Decisions felt like educated guesses rather than confident moves.

The board approved the deployment of an AI-driven financial intelligence system, and within weeks, Isabel noticed something different. The company no longer closed its books at the end of the month. There was nothing to close. The numbers were always current. The system displayed rolling forecasts that updated every time a shipment moved, an invoice was paid, or a regulation changed. Profit was no longer a mystery—it was a moving target that the system tracked constantly.

Midway through the first quarter, the AI CFO issued a subtle alert. While revenue was on track, the system detected a pattern forming in fuel costs and regional tax exposure that would compress margins by the end of the quarter. In the past, Isabel would not have seen this until weeks after the damage was done. Now she had time. The system suggested three options: adjust pricing in specific regions, renegotiate supplier contracts, or shift routing to reduce tax friction. Isabel reviewed the scenarios and approved a hybrid approach. The changes were implemented automatically across the organization.

As weeks passed, Isabel watched the forecast stabilize. The margin compression disappeared before it ever reached the income statement. When the quarter ended, there was no scramble, no emergency meeting, no shocked expressions around the boardroom table. The results were exactly as predicted. For the first time in the company's history, the quarter ended without surprises.

Later that year, an economic shock rippled through the industry. Competitors reacted with layoffs and panic. Isabel's system had already modeled the scenario months earlier. She had adjusted spending gradually, preserved cash, and positioned the company to absorb the impact. While others scrambled, her company continued operating smoothly.

One evening, Isabel reflected on how different leadership felt. She was no longer reacting to problems—she was preventing them. The AI CFO did not replace her instincts, but it sharpened them. The future was no longer something that happened to the company. It was something the company could see, shape, and optimize in advance.

Chapter 7

The Autonomous Enterprise and the Disappearance of Financial Fear

For as long as businesses have existed, financial fear has been a constant companion. Fear of running out of cash. Fear of unexpected taxes. Fear of audits. Fear of regulatory mistakes. Fear of making the wrong strategic move at the wrong time. Even successful companies often operate under a persistent sense of uncertainty because their financial systems are reactive, fragmented, and incomplete. Artificial intelligence changes this dynamic completely. As AI-driven tax, accounting, forecasting, and compliance systems converge, they give rise to the autonomous enterprise—an organization that can operate, adapt, and optimize itself financially with minimal human intervention. In this environment, financial fear does not disappear because risks vanish, but because risks become visible, measurable, and manageable in real time.

The autonomous enterprise is defined by continuous financial awareness. Every transaction, contract, payroll event, asset movement, and tax obligation is tracked, interpreted, and evaluated instantly. Instead of waiting for reports, leaders operate inside a living financial model that reflects reality as it unfolds. This eliminates the anxiety that comes from not knowing where the business truly stands. When cash flow, tax exposure, compliance status, and profitability are always visible, uncertainty gives way to confidence. Decisions stop feeling like gambles and start feeling like calculated moves grounded in data.

One of the most transformative aspects of the autonomous enterprise is its ability to self-correct. Traditional organizations rely on periodic reviews to identify problems, often discovering issues long after they have caused damage. AI-driven systems detect deviations the moment they begin to form. If expenses rise faster than revenue, the system flags it immediately. If tax exposure increases in a particular jurisdiction, it adjusts strategy proactively. If compliance risk grows due to regulatory changes or operational drift, the system responds before enforcement becomes an issue. This constant self-regulation prevents small problems from turning into existential threats.

Autonomy also changes how businesses experience regulation. Instead of viewing tax authorities and regulators as external threats, autonomous enterprises integrate compliance directly into their operations. Rules are enforced automatically through AI, smart contracts, and digital reporting systems. This removes the fear of missing deadlines, misinterpreting laws, or failing audits. Compliance becomes a background process rather than a recurring crisis. Businesses are no longer reacting to regulations—they are aligned with them by design.

Another critical shift is the emotional impact on leadership. Financial fear consumes cognitive energy. It forces executives to spend time worrying instead of creating. When AI systems handle forecasting, optimization, and compliance continuously, leaders regain mental space. They can think long-term, invest strategically, and pursue innovation without constant anxiety about financial surprises. This psychological shift is just as important as the operational benefits. Confident leaders make better decisions, take smarter risks, and build more resilient organizations.

The autonomous enterprise also redefines accountability. In traditional systems, errors are often blamed on individuals—an accountant missed something, a manager made a mistake, a report was wrong. In an AI-driven system, responsibility shifts to process and design. Errors become signals that the system needs adjustment rather than evidence of human failure. This fosters a healthier organizational culture focused on improvement rather than blame. Teams trust the system, and the system continuously improves through feedback and learning.

As autonomy increases, businesses gain the ability to operate at scale without proportional increases in overhead. Growth no longer multiplies complexity because AI absorbs it. Whether a company doubles in size, expands into new markets, or adds new revenue streams, the financial system scales seamlessly. This removes one of the biggest constraints on growth and allows companies to pursue opportunities that would have been too risky or complex in the past.

Ultimately, the autonomous enterprise represents a new stage of organizational evolution. Just as automation transformed manufacturing and software transformed communication, AI transforms financial management. Businesses become adaptive systems capable of sensing, responding, and optimizing continuously. Financial fear fades because the unknown becomes known, the unpredictable becomes modeled, and the chaotic becomes structured. This does not make business effortless—but it makes it intelligible.

The companies that embrace autonomy will define the next era of commerce. They will move faster, operate more efficiently, and withstand shocks that cripple less intelligent organizations. They will attract better talent, better capital, and better partners because confidence is contagious. In a world of accelerating complexity, autonomy is not a luxury—it is a survival strategy.

The Day the Fear Lifted

For years, Thomas carried a quiet weight that never left him. Even when his manufacturing company posted record revenues, even when new contracts rolled in, the fear was always there. It sat behind every decision, whispering doubts. What if cash flow tightened unexpectedly? What if a tax rule changed? What if an audit uncovered something he didn't know existed? Thomas slept lightly, woke early, and checked his finances obsessively, searching for reassurance that never fully came.

When his board approved the transition to a fully autonomous financial system, Thomas was skeptical. He trusted people, not machines. He trusted experience, not algorithms. But the old way was exhausting him, and he knew something had to change. The system went live quietly, without ceremony. There was no dramatic announcement, no grand reveal. It simply began connecting itself to everything—banks, suppliers, payroll, inventory, tax authorities—building a real-time financial model of the company that never stopped updating.

At first, Thomas checked the dashboard constantly, expecting to find errors or inconsistencies. Instead, he found clarity. Cash flow projections updated with every shipment. Tax obligations adjusted automatically as sales crossed jurisdictional thresholds. Compliance scores remained steady, even as regulations shifted. The system did not overwhelm him with data; it distilled complexity into insight. For the first time, Thomas could see his business as it truly was, not as a collection of delayed reports, but as a living, breathing organism.

Months passed, and something unexpected happened. The fear began to fade. Not all at once, but gradually, like fog lifting in the morning sun. When a supplier raised prices, the system flagged the impact immediately and proposed alternatives. When a new tax regulation passed, compliance updated automatically without panic. When revenue dipped in one region, the system compensated elsewhere through optimization. Problems still existed, but they were never surprises.

Then came the real test. A global economic shock hit the industry, triggering supply chain disruptions and market uncertainty. Competitors reacted with layoffs, emergency loans, and frantic restructuring. Thomas watched his dashboard as the system simulated multiple scenarios in real time. It adjusted inventory levels, renegotiated supplier terms through automated contracts, optimized tax timing, and preserved cash flow. There were no emergency meetings, no sleepless nights. The company bent without breaking. One evening, long after the crisis had passed, Thomas sat alone in his office and realized something profound. For the first time in his career, he was not afraid of his own business. The fear that had shadowed him for decades was gone, replaced by trust—not blind trust, but informed trust in a system that saw more, reacted faster, and optimized continuously. He understood then that autonomy was not about surrendering control. It was about gaining clarity so complete that fear no longer had room to exist.

As he shut down the lights and walked out, Thomas smiled quietly. The numbers were still there. The risks were still real. But the fear was gone—and in its absence, possibility finally felt limitless.

Chapter 8

From Compliance to Competitive Advantage: How AI Turns Taxes Into Power

For most businesses, taxation has always been treated as a necessary burden—something to endure, minimize, and move past as quickly as possible. Compliance was defensive, reactive, and disconnected from strategy. Artificial intelligence fundamentally reverses this relationship. In an AI-powered financial ecosystem, taxes are no longer just an obligation; they become a source of competitive advantage. Chapter 8 explores how businesses that fully integrate AI-driven tax intelligence, compliance automation, and predictive optimization transform taxation from a cost center into a strategic weapon that strengthens margins, accelerates growth, and widens the gap between leaders and laggards.

The shift begins when compliance stops being periodic and becomes continuous. In traditional systems, businesses comply retroactively, assembling records after transactions are complete and hoping nothing was missed. AI replaces this with real-time enforcement, ensuring that every transaction is structured optimally at the moment it occurs. This prevents inefficiencies before they happen rather than correcting them later. Over time, the cumulative effect of thousands of optimized micro-decisions produces a massive advantage. Companies pay the right amount of tax, at the right time, in the right jurisdiction—no more and no less. This precision alone can mean millions in retained capital compared to competitors operating blindly.

AI-driven tax systems also unlock strategic timing advantages. Taxes are not just about how much you pay, but *when* you pay. AI continuously models cash flow, revenue recognition, expense timing, depreciation schedules, and credit utilization to determine the most advantageous timing for every financial move. By smoothing tax payments, accelerating deductions, and aligning liabilities with revenue cycles, businesses improve liquidity without increasing risk. This allows them to reinvest faster, respond to opportunities sooner, and weather downturns with greater resilience. Competitors stuck in static systems often do not realize they are at a disadvantage until it is too late.

Another powerful advantage emerges in pricing and market expansion. AI allows businesses to model after-tax profitability at the product, customer, and regional level in real time. Companies can see exactly which offerings generate the highest net profit after taxes and compliance costs. This insight informs smarter pricing strategies, targeted expansion, and faster exit from unprofitable markets. Instead of relying on gross margins or high-level averages, leaders operate with precise, tax-aware intelligence that reveals where real value is created. This level of clarity is nearly impossible to achieve manually at scale.

AI also enables what can be called compliance signaling—a subtle but powerful advantage in competitive markets. Businesses with transparent, real-time compliance records are more attractive to investors, lenders, partners, and acquirers. When financial and tax data is continuously verified and audit-ready, due diligence becomes faster and less risky. Deals close sooner. Financing terms improve. Strategic partnerships become easier to secure. Compliance stops being a hidden liability and becomes a visible asset that signals operational maturity and reliability.

As AI systems learn from enforcement trends and regulatory behavior, they also help businesses avoid strategies that may be technically legal but practically risky. Instead of pushing aggressive positions that invite scrutiny, AI identifies optimization paths that are both effective and defensible. This reduces the likelihood of disputes, audits, and reputational damage. Over time, companies develop a reputation for clean, intelligent compliance, which further reduces regulatory friction and enforcement intensity. In effect, AI helps businesses stay ahead of regulators by aligning with how rules are actually applied, not just how they are written.

Perhaps the most transformative aspect of AI-driven tax advantage is scalability. Traditional tax strategies often break down as businesses grow, expand internationally, or add complexity. AI systems thrive on complexity. They become more accurate as data volume increases and more valuable as operations expand. This allows businesses to scale without proportional increases in tax risk or administrative overhead. Growth becomes cleaner, faster, and more predictable, giving AI-enabled companies a structural advantage that compounds over time.

This dynamic creates a widening gap in the marketplace. Businesses that adopt AI-driven tax intelligence early gain efficiency, liquidity, and strategic clarity that competitors cannot easily replicate. Late adopters face higher costs, slower decision-making, and greater exposure to compliance risk. Over time, this gap becomes self-reinforcing. The leaders reinvest their savings into growth and innovation, while others struggle to keep up. Taxes, once seen as a drag on performance, become a force multiplier for those who understand how to harness them. In the future economy, competitive advantage will not come only from better products or marketing, but from superior financial intelligence. AI-powered taxation sits at the center of this shift. It transforms compliance into insight, insight into strategy, and strategy into sustained dominance. Businesses that embrace this reality will not just survive the transition to digital finance—they will define it.

The Quiet Advantage

When Leah founded her consumer goods company, she believed competition would be loud. She expected rivals to outspend her on marketing, undercut her on price, or outmaneuver her with flashy technology. What she did not expect was that her greatest advantage would be invisible. While competitors fought for attention, Leah invested quietly in something far less glamorous: an AI-driven financial and tax intelligence system that embedded itself into every decision her company made.

At first, the difference was subtle. Her cash flow felt smoother. Tax payments never surprised her. Quarterly results aligned closely with forecasts. She assumed this was simply good management. But as the company expanded into new regions, the contrast became impossible to ignore. Competitors hesitated, delayed launches, and pulled back from markets after discovering unexpected tax friction. Leah's system had already modeled those markets months earlier. It adjusted pricing, structured operations efficiently, and flagged the most profitable paths forward. By the time others reacted, Leah was already established.

One year later, an acquisition opportunity emerged. A larger competitor wanted to buy Leah's company, impressed by its steady growth and strong margins. During due diligence, something unexpected happened. The acquiring firm's analysts moved quickly through Leah's financials—not because they were simple, but because they were clean. Every number was verifiable. Every tax position was defensible. Every forecast matched historical performance with uncanny accuracy. What usually took months took weeks. The offer that followed included a premium Leah had not anticipated.

Leah declined.

Instead, she watched as the acquiring firm struggled. Its own systems were fragmented. Tax liabilities surfaced late. Compliance issues slowed expansion. Meanwhile, Leah's company continued to grow quietly, steadily, and profitably. She reinvested savings from optimized tax timing into product development. She used liquidity advantages to negotiate better supplier terms. She expanded into markets others avoided because her system showed her how to do it safely.

Years later, Leah attended an industry conference where executives openly discussed the challenges of rising compliance costs and regulatory complexity. She listened politely, knowing that her company faced the same environment—but experienced it very differently. For her, taxes were not a threat. They were a guide. Her AI system continuously adjusted her course, keeping her aligned, efficient, and ahead of the curve.

On the flight home, Leah reviewed her dashboard as the system simulated the next five years of growth. The path forward was clear, not because the future was predictable, but because it was modeled, monitored, and optimized every day. She realized then that true competitive advantage rarely announces itself. It operates quietly, compounding in the background, until one day it becomes impossible to catch.

Chapter 9

Resilience by Design: How AI Builds Tax-Safe, Shock-Proof Businesses

Every business leader eventually learns the same hard lesson: it is not growth that destroys companies, but shocks. Sudden regulatory changes. Economic downturns. Cash-flow freezes. Tax reassessments. Audits triggered at the worst possible time. Historically, resilience was built through buffers—extra cash, conservative growth, and human oversight. Artificial intelligence introduces an entirely new model of resilience, one that is proactive, adaptive, and designed directly into the financial architecture of the business. In this chapter, we explore how AI transforms taxation and financial systems into shock-absorbing structures that allow companies not only to survive disruption, but to emerge stronger because of it.

Traditional tax and accounting systems are brittle. They operate on delayed inputs, static assumptions, and periodic reconciliation. When a shock occurs, leaders often discover vulnerabilities long after corrective action is possible. AI replaces this fragility with continuous sensing. It monitors the internal state of the business and the external environment simultaneously—tracking revenue volatility, regulatory updates, enforcement behavior, liquidity stress, supplier risk, currency exposure, and tax policy shifts in real time. This allows the system to detect early signals of disruption before they escalate into crises. Resilience begins not with reaction, but with anticipation.

AI-driven tax systems play a critical role in this anticipatory defense. Taxes are one of the most common sources of financial shock because liabilities often surface late and in concentrated amounts. AI prevents this by distributing tax awareness across time. Instead of discovering exposure at filing deadlines, the system models tax obligations continuously, stress-testing scenarios under different revenue levels, regulatory interpretations, and enforcement trends. If a future liability threatens liquidity, the system flags it early and proposes mitigation strategies—adjusting timing, restructuring transactions, or reallocating cash proactively. Shock is replaced by controlled adjustment.

Another pillar of AI-driven resilience is diversification awareness. Businesses often believe they are diversified because they operate across products or markets, but tax and regulatory exposure can remain dangerously concentrated. AI evaluates diversification not just at the revenue level, but at the after-tax, after-compliance level. It identifies hidden concentrations—such as reliance on a single jurisdiction's tax incentives, exposure to one enforcement regime, or dependency on specific deductions that may disappear. By revealing these structural weaknesses, AI allows businesses to rebalance before disruption forces painful decisions.

Resilience also depends on speed. In a crisis, the businesses that survive are those that act first and with clarity. AI eliminates the delays caused by manual analysis, incomplete data, and internal debate over numbers. When conditions change, the system recalculates forecasts instantly and presents leaders with ranked options, each showing financial, tax, and compliance impact. This compresses decision cycles dramatically. Leaders move from weeks to hours, from speculation to evidence, and from panic to control.

Regulatory shocks are particularly dangerous because they often arrive without warning and affect entire industries simultaneously. AI systems continuously monitor legislative pipelines, regulatory commentary, enforcement actions, and court rulings. They do not wait for laws to be finalized. Instead, they model likely outcomes and prepare the business in advance. When changes become official, adjustments are already in place. Compliance transitions from a scramble to a smooth handoff, preserving stability while competitors struggle to adapt. Financial resilience is also psychological. Leaders who operate without clear financial visibility experience chronic stress that degrades judgment over time.

AI restores clarity by making uncertainty measurable. Instead of vague fears about audits, tax exposure, or cash shortfalls, leaders see quantified risks with probability ranges and mitigation paths. This reduces emotional decision-making and allows leadership teams to stay calm under pressure. Calm leaders make better decisions, and better decisions compound into resilience.

AI-driven systems also enable what can be called graceful degradation. When shocks are severe and unavoidable, resilient businesses do not collapse—they contract intelligently. AI identifies which costs can be reduced with minimal long-term damage, which investments must be protected, and which tax strategies can preserve liquidity during contraction. Rather than blunt cuts, the system guides precision adjustments that maintain core strength. This ability to bend without breaking is the hallmark of resilient organizations.

Over time, resilience becomes self-reinforcing. Businesses that absorb shocks smoothly gain confidence, credibility, and trust—from investors, regulators, partners, and employees. Capital becomes cheaper. Partnerships become easier. Regulatory scrutiny decreases. Each successful response to disruption strengthens the system's learning models, making the next response even better. Resilience stops being a defensive posture and becomes a competitive asset. In the AI-powered future, resilience is not built through fear or conservatism. It is engineered through intelligence. Tax systems are no longer hidden liabilities waiting to explode under pressure. They become stabilizers that distribute risk, smooth volatility, and protect cash flow continuously. Businesses designed this way do not merely survive uncertainty—they are built for it.

The Storm That Didn't Break Them

When the shock finally came, it arrived the way all real shocks do—quietly at first. No alarms. No headlines. Just a change buried deep inside a regulatory update that most companies would not notice until months later. For Daniel Reyes, CEO of a mid-sized international logistics firm, the change would have been devastating in another life. A reinterpretation of cross-border service taxation threatened to retroactively increase liabilities across three major markets. For many of Daniel's competitors, it would trigger audits, frozen cash, and emergency layoffs.

Daniel did not hear about it from a lawyer. He did not read about it in the news. His AI system detected it within hours.

The alert was calm, almost understated. A probability shift. A projected liability curve bending upward six months into the future. A confidence score showing increased enforcement likelihood based on historical patterns. Daniel opened the dashboard and saw what the system already knew: if nothing changed, the company would face a severe cash squeeze at the worst possible time of year.

But panic never arrived.

The AI had already modeled the shock. It presented options—each one simulated across tax exposure, cash flow, compliance risk, and operational impact. One option involved restructuring service contracts. Another involved shifting revenue recognition timing. A third involved re-routing certain operations through jurisdictions with reciprocal agreements. None were aggressive. All were defensible. The system ranked them not by savings alone, but by resilience.

Daniel convened his leadership team. The conversation felt different from past crises. No one argued about the numbers. No one questioned the data. The uncertainty had already been absorbed by the models. They chose a blended approach, and the system began executing adjustments automatically—updating contracts, notifying partners, adjusting tax logic, and reallocating cash buffers.

Weeks passed. Then months.

Competitors began to struggle. News broke of audits. Emergency capital raises. Sudden workforce reductions. Daniel watched it unfold with a strange sense of detachment. His company felt insulated, not because the shock was small, but because it had been distributed. Tax liabilities never arrived in a lump. Cash flow remained stable. Compliance scores stayed high.

Then the real test came.

An industry-wide downturn followed the regulatory shock, compounding pressure across supply chains. Even well-run companies faltered. Daniel's AI system shifted again—this time focusing on graceful contraction. It identified non-critical spend that could be paused without long-term damage. It protected investments tied to future growth. It adjusted tax timing to preserve liquidity. The company slowed, but it did not stumble.

One evening, long after the storm had passed, Daniel stood alone in the office, looking at a five-year forecast projected calmly on the screen. The company was still standing. Still profitable. Still trusted by regulators and partners alike. He realized that resilience had not come from strength alone, but from intelligence embedded everywhere.

The storm had been real. The danger had been real. But the business had been built for uncertainty, not surprised by it. And in that quiet realization, Daniel understood something few leaders ever do until it is too late: resilience is not about surviving the storm—it is about never being caught unaware by it again.

Chapter 10

The Zero-Friction Economy: Where Taxes, Accounting, and Business Fully Disappear Into Intelligence

The final stage of AI-powered business taxation is not optimization, automation, or even autonomy—it is disappearance. In the zero-friction economy, taxes, accounting, and compliance do not vanish because they are ignored, but because they are so deeply integrated into intelligent systems that they no longer register as separate activities. Just as modern users no longer think about how data packets move across the internet, future business leaders will not think about filing taxes, reconciling books, or preparing for audits. These functions dissolve into background intelligence that operates continuously, invisibly, and flawlessly. Chapter 10 explores what happens when financial friction reaches zero—and how this reshapes business, government, and economic power itself.

Zero friction begins when financial intelligence becomes ambient. AI no longer sits inside isolated tools or dashboards; it becomes embedded across every layer of commerce. Contracts are written with tax logic already encoded. Payments move through systems that understand jurisdiction, classification, and compliance automatically. Assets depreciate themselves based on real usage data. Revenue recognizes itself according to live regulatory interpretation. In this environment, accounting does not happen *after* business—it happens *as* business. The distinction disappears entirely.

This shift radically alters the speed of economic activity. When taxes and compliance no longer slow decisions, businesses move at the pace of intention rather than administration. New markets can be entered instantly because regulatory alignment is automatic. Partnerships form faster because financial trust is verified in real time. Capital flows more efficiently because risk is continuously priced and monitored. Entire layers of delay—approval cycles, reconciliations, audits, filings—collapse into milliseconds of computation. The economy accelerates not through recklessness, but through clarity.

Governments evolve alongside this transformation. In a zero-friction economy, tax authorities no longer act as collectors chasing revenue after the fact. They become system designers, embedding fiscal policy directly into digital infrastructure. Tax rates, incentives, and enforcement rules are expressed as machine-readable logic that updates automatically when policy changes. Compliance becomes systemic rather than behavioral. Governments gain unprecedented revenue stability while dramatically reducing enforcement costs. The political tension around taxation shifts, because disputes about interpretation and reporting largely disappear.

For businesses, the disappearance of friction fundamentally changes strategic thinking. When financial systems are always correct and always current, leaders stop budgeting for error, delay, and uncertainty. They plan with confidence. They allocate capital based on true after-tax outcomes. They measure performance by real economic value rather than accounting artifacts. Strategy becomes cleaner, faster, and more aligned with reality. The competitive landscape reshapes itself around intelligence rather than scale alone.

This also democratizes sophisticated financial management. In the past, zero-friction-like efficiency was reserved for the largest corporations with massive compliance budgets. AI makes it available to startups, solo founders, and small enterprises. A one-person company can now operate with the financial sophistication of a multinational, because intelligence—not headcount—does the work. This levels the playing field and unleashes a new wave of entrepreneurship unburdened by administrative overhead.

As friction disappears, trust increases. Investors trust numbers that are continuously verified. Regulators trust systems that enforce rules automatically. Partners trust contracts that execute predictably. Customers trust businesses that operate transparently. This trust compounds, reducing the need for defensive processes and accelerating collaboration. The economy becomes less adversarial and more aligned, because intelligence resolves disputes before they arise.

Critically, the zero-friction economy does not eliminate human judgment—it elevates it. When machines handle complexity, humans focus on vision, ethics, creativity, and leadership. Business leaders spend less time worrying about compliance and more time shaping outcomes. Governments focus less on enforcement and more on policy design. The relationship between humans and systems becomes cooperative rather than burdensome.

In this final state, taxation is no longer perceived as extraction, accounting as bureaucracy, or compliance as fear. They become neutral, intelligent mechanisms that support economic flow. Businesses operate inside guardrails that are invisible yet firm. Growth accelerates without chaos. Innovation flourishes without risk blindness. The system becomes resilient not because it resists change, but because it adapts instantly.

The zero-friction economy represents the endpoint of the transformation explored throughout this series. It is not a fantasy or a distant future. Its components already exist—AI, real-time data, digital governments, smart contracts, predictive systems. What remains is adoption, integration, and mindset. Businesses that understand this future will build effortlessly within it. Those that do not will experience the remaining friction as an ever-increasing disadvantage.

In the end, the goal of AI-powered taxation is not to make businesses think more about taxes—but to make them think about them not at all. When intelligence is complete, friction disappears. And when friction disappears, what remains is pure execution, clarity, and opportunity.

The Day Business Became Effortless

The first sign that something had changed was how quiet it felt.

No alerts.No deadlines.No reminders.

For Sofia Mendes, founder of a global digital services firm, the absence was unsettling at first. For years, her calendar had been filled with financial checkpoints—quarterly estimates, compliance reviews, filing windows, audit prep meetings. Even after adopting advanced AI systems, those rituals had merely become faster. Now they were gone entirely.

Not postponed.Not automated.Gone. Her company's systems no longer asked her to approve tax payments. They no longer requested reconciliations. They no longer flagged compliance tasks. Everything simply... flowed. Revenue arrived, expenses moved, employees were paid, assets adjusted, taxes settled themselves quietly in the background.

Sofia watched the dashboard—not because it demanded attention, but because she was curious. Every number was live. Every projection was stable. The future no longer felt opaque; it felt continuously visible.

Then an opportunity appeared.

A government-backed infrastructure project opened unexpectedly in three countries at once. In the past, Sofia would have hesitated. Multi-jurisdiction tax exposure. Compliance risk. Currency treatment. Reporting complexity. Even with AI, expansion used to require planning cycles measured in weeks.

This time, she clicked once.

Her systems analyzed the jurisdictions, mapped the tax logic, adjusted contracts, aligned reporting standards, and priced the project after tax in real time. What used to be an expansion plan was now a decision. The contracts executed themselves. Payments routed correctly. Compliance embedded itself automatically.

By the time her competitors scheduled meetings, Sofia's company was already operating.

Weeks later, an investor reached out—not with questions, but with an offer. During due diligence, there were no document requests. No reconciliations. No clarifications. The investor accessed a verified, continuous financial stream that told the complete story of the business without explanation. Risk was visible. Profit was predictable. Trust was instant.

Sofia declined again.

Not because the offer wasn't good—but because the business no longer felt heavy. It no longer felt fragile. It no longer required defensive thinking. Growth had become smooth, almost inevitable, because nothing slowed it down.

One evening, Sofia sat alone, reflecting on the early years—the stress, the fear, the endless vigilance. She realized that the hardest part of running a business had never been competition or innovation. It had been friction. The constant drag of systems that lagged behind reality.

Now, those systems were gone.

Business no longer demanded attention to survive. It responded intelligently, continuously, without complaint. Sofia wasn't managing complexity anymore—she was shaping direction.

As she shut down her screen, she understood the truth that would define the next era of commerce:

The future didn't belong to the biggest companies.It belonged to the least burdened ones.

And for the first time, business felt effortless—not because it was easy, but because intelligence had finally removed everything that never needed to exist in the first place.

Final Thoughts

The End of Friction, the Beginning of Intelligent Enterprise

As this book—and the entire ten-book professional series—comes to a close, one truth stands above all others: business taxation has reached a permanent point of no return. Artificial intelligence has not merely improved how taxes are calculated, reported, or optimized; it has fundamentally changed what taxation *is*. What was once a periodic, fear-driven, paperwork-heavy obligation has evolved into a continuous, intelligent, and largely invisible system woven directly into the fabric of modern commerce. The implications of this shift extend far beyond accounting departments or tax filings. They redefine how businesses grow, how governments govern, and how economic power is distributed in the digital age.

For decades, business owners were conditioned to accept friction as normal. Delays were expected. Uncertainty was tolerated. Surprise tax bills, audits, compliance errors, and cash-flow shocks were treated as unavoidable costs of doing business. Entire industries emerged to manage this friction—consultants, auditors, compliance specialists, and legal teams whose primary role was to navigate complexity created by outdated systems. AI does not simply reduce this friction; it renders much of it obsolete. When intelligence operates continuously, there is no longer a gap between action and understanding. The lag that once created fear disappears, and with it, the emotional and financial toll that defined traditional business operations.

Throughout this series, we have seen how AI replaces hindsight with foresight. Taxes are no longer discovered after profits are earned; they are modeled before decisions are made. Compliance is no longer verified months or years later; it is enforced in real time. Risk is no longer something businesses stumble into unknowingly; it is quantified, monitored, and managed continuously. This shift alone represents one of the most significant advances in business resilience in modern history. Companies stop being reactive entities and become adaptive systems—capable of sensing change, responding intelligently, and optimizing themselves without constant human intervention.

Perhaps the most profound transformation explored in this book is psychological rather than technical. Financial fear has shaped leadership behavior for generations. Executives learned to be cautious not because caution was strategic, but because uncertainty demanded it. AI removes much of that uncertainty. When leaders can see accurate, real-time, forward-looking financial information at all times, decision-making changes. Confidence replaces anxiety. Strategy replaces guesswork. Long-term thinking replaces short-term survival tactics. This shift in mindset is what ultimately separates businesses that merely adopt AI tools from those that truly become AI-driven organizations.

The convergence of AI with digital governments, blockchain verification, smart contracts, and predictive analytics signals a future where taxation is no longer a battlefield between businesses and regulators. Instead, it becomes a shared system of truth. Governments gain stability, accuracy, and efficiency. Businesses gain clarity, fairness, and predictability. Enforcement shifts from punishment to prevention. Disputes shrink because data replaces interpretation. The adversarial model of taxation gives way to a collaborative digital infrastructure where compliance is built in by design.

Importantly, this future is not reserved for massive corporations or elite institutions. One of AI's greatest contributions is democratization. A solo entrepreneur with the right systems can now operate with the financial sophistication of a multinational enterprise. Real-time tax intelligence, automated compliance, predictive forecasting, and optimization are no longer luxuries—they are increasingly standard features of modern financial platforms. This levels the competitive landscape and opens the door to a new era of entrepreneurship, where innovation is limited less by administrative burden and more by imagination and execution.

Yet this transformation also carries responsibility. As financial systems become more autonomous, the role of human judgment does not disappear—it evolves. Ethics, governance, and intent matter more than ever. AI can optimize within any framework it is given, which means businesses and governments alike must be intentional about the values they encode into these systems. Transparency, fairness, and accountability must be designed into the architecture of intelligent finance, not assumed as byproducts. The future described in this book is powerful, but power must be guided thoughtfully.

Looking ahead, the businesses that will thrive are not those that simply "use AI," but those that reorganize themselves around intelligence. They will design operations where data flows freely, systems learn continuously, and decisions are made with full awareness of consequence. They will treat taxes not as an afterthought, but as an integrated element of strategy—optimized quietly, continuously, and defensibly. Over time, these businesses will appear effortless from the outside, not because they face fewer challenges, but because friction no longer slows their response.

For those still operating in manual, fragmented, or reactive financial systems, the gap will widen. Friction compounds just as intelligence does. Delays become disadvantages. Uncertainty becomes risk. Complexity becomes cost. This is not a moral judgment; it is a structural reality of the digital economy. Adoption of AI-driven tax and financial systems is no longer about gaining an edge—it is about remaining viable as the baseline of business operations shifts.

In closing, the future of AI-powered business taxation is not about eliminating responsibility or oversight. It is about eliminating unnecessary struggle. It is about aligning economic activity with real-time truth. It is about allowing businesses to focus on creating value rather than navigating chaos. When intelligence is embedded deeply enough, taxes stop being something you manage and start being something that simply works.

The ultimate promise of this transformation is freedom—not freedom from paying taxes, but freedom from fear, confusion, and inefficiency. Freedom to build with confidence. Freedom to grow without constant friction. Freedom to operate in a system that understands you as well as you understand your business.

That future is not speculative. It is already arriving.

And the businesses that step into it now will not just adapt to the next era of commerce—they will define it.

www.ingramcontent.com/pod-product-compliance
Ingram Content Group UK Ltd.
Pitfield, Milton Keynes, MK11 3LW, UK
UKHW020157290926
15471UKWH00005B/916

9 798295 593444